www.coachdana.biz

Introduction

Everybody believes that money will cure all of their problems when in actuality it won't. Whatever problems you had before you had an abundance of money you will still have; it comes down to mindset and training. Where in the world did you learn how to spend or how not to spend the money you have? (Or lack there of) What will change your mindset so that you are in a better place to receive and give?
B.A.D.(Blessed, Anointed & Destined)Money gives you an inside look at how I was trained and the mindset I had and how to change that so you don't have to go through it. Are you ready? We can surly do this together.
Dana Neal, Author/Coach

Where I received my Training

www.coachdana.biz

Copyright/Terms of Use:

All information contained in this book is copyrighted 2013, 2014 by C.K.Q. LLC. All rights are reserved.

You may not sell this book for any price. You may not publish any portions of this book. You may not edit this book in anyway. You may not put this book on your website. You may not rewrite, sell, publish or distribute this book in any way without permission of the author.

www.coachdana.biz

Table of Contents

Introduction……………………3

Chapter 1: Where I Received My training………………………..4

Chapter 2: Living and Investing Paycheck to Paycheck……….11

Chapter 3: Bankruptcy Isn't the Option……………………….22

Chapter 4: God wants you to Have Wealth………………………27

Chapter 5: From Victim to Victor ………………………………34

About the Author …………..38

My mother always talked about how I didn't know how to count money properly. Never, really showed me how to count money, as a child, she just said I couldn't do it; not smart enough. The troublesome part about it is that I would try and she would get frustrated in my trying. Nonetheless, that is where I started my training.

I was told to save money. I was taught how to work for my allowance, and what would happen if I didn't do what I was told. (Basic math was not part of this early training.) I was also only given just enough, and that just enough was NOT enough. For example, at 14, in the 80's, my allowance was $20-$25 dollars every two weeks. I had to purchase a weekly bus pass, which was about $7, I had to get my hair done (which I hardly ever did) and then try to have fun (movies, mall etc) which most times, I couldn't. I was being trained to want more before I could even enjoy what I had.

The one thing I learned in this 'training', as a youth, was that I could bargain shop. I found discounts on lip gloss, shoes, etc. The only thing was getting my hair done. Once every six weeks for a touch up and then maintain at home. I had to make my little allowance work. I also learned how to search for and ask for sales. The problem here is, I was fourteen; truly behind the times when my other friends were ahead of the game. My girl friends parents always made sure they had. You would think I would be an extreme couponer or robbing banks. I'm literally straight down the middle.

By the time I had my own children and my own income, I was spending what I had and what I didn't! I was more in debt after my first child than I was ever broke in my teenage years. After my first year of college, I was offered and approved for my very first credit card. I truly thought I was something! I was broker than broke faster than fast. (This is your opportunity to laugh.) I am still wondering why I did that to myself.

It was how I was trained.

In my mind, I wanted to get the money, didn't care about making the money; didn't care about not having any payments; I just wanted to have diapers, new clothes and things for my daughter. I was inadvertently trained to WANT and however I had to GET what I wanted was the best decision I could make.

That training had me going down hill. I was a victim of want. I was a victim of desires. I was a victim of trying to have what I couldn't afford. I wasn't trained to get what I could afford.

In actuality, I can't even say what kind of training it really was; I mean I was never taught to tithe; never taught to save; I was taught to use what I had to the best of my ability. At a young age, I saw little money and wanted more. I can praise God that I didn't learn to rob banks, break in houses, or steal from others. But I never had what I wanted or needed. My training was a mix of everything that was unstable. The training was what I was being told not what I was being taught.

What does this mean for you?

This means that you really have to look over your life and find out where you missed the mark financially. Were you busted and disgusted with your allowance? Did you work really hard only to get a little and then you had to make that work for everything you needed? Truly step back from your current situation and see what you were taught all those years ago. Those lessons are hidden in your financial mindset right now; the victim-ology was embedded in your mind as a child. You were never told that you could control the money to benefit you; the money controlled you.

Living and Investing Paycheck to Paycheck

My mother who was a very good budgeter and a person, who could save money very well, was one who paid her house off in 15 years instead of 30, and has trained herself how to pay for everything in cash. I hadn't learned THAT PART yet, but I see a trend here from my childhood to my children in theirs.

I am looking at the fact that I wanted cash for myself so bad, that I trained my children to do and want the same. It's bad when you have young adults and teenagers that have acquired that in their lives, because now I am trying to change my mindset and instill that in them. I truly feel that I have to step back and let them watch me re-teach myself. It's a funny thing right now in our lives. None the less, this was where I learned my lesson, however positive; the reverse is what has happened in my life.

My mind was set on going paycheck to paycheck.

I know you are probably thinking how in the world this chapter makes any sense. Well, it doesn't, but it's factual for the lesson that has to be learned. You are B.A.D.; the key term here is DESTINED!

I was going paycheck to paycheck and was very excited that I had a job and money to look forward to every week. It wasn't until recently, while going through an online training with my coach, that I was taking that bi-weekly pay for granted. I was working my business as if that money was going to always be there.

Okay, let's pause right here: I'm a serial entrepreneur. I've been building a business without support or help for over twelve years and I'm still trying to go back to my small business why and that is to be available for my children. If I can get away from the understanding of having a paycheck every two weeks, then I get closer to make that second million. Okay back to the lessons.

The fact was, the money was coming in but also being spent just as fast at it was deposited. If I can just go back about 6 years, I was doing some radical things with my money and truly trying to justify my spending. In actuality, I can only justify it as investing into myself and growing my business, but at the time, it wasn't growing. The seeds being sown were being stuck in the mud and not taking root. Seeds, if watered properly and in the right soil, should take root and grow, and these didn't.

The investments didn't leave me with a total bad taste in my mouth; I saw how to redirect the lessons learned into things that were best for my entrepreneurial future and business growth. BUT, I was still living paycheck to paycheck. What was the problem? Where was my financial mindset six years ago that wasn't changing even after realizing the questionable investments were made? I was leaning on the bi-weekly money like it would always be there. I was never considering that things would ever change.

For years my bank account was suffering from a negative balance right before the next check would be deposited. I just figured all will work out. I just kept leaning on that money. Why am I saying this? When we accept what isn't even the norm, we get comfortable in what is wrong and that's not right; it's another form of bondage and *victimology; the blessings were being missed.* We are not victims; we are victors; YOU'RE B.A.D. POINT BLANK PERIOD.

Now, going back to those six years prior, I have to say in the middle of all of that, I suffered the consequences of my actions. Being broke for at least 3 days before the next pay day. Not being able to afford gas in my vehicle, lunch money for my children, or even lunch money for myself. There were times, as we get closer to the last 3 years, that I couldn't pay my life insurance policies, I only had one week's worth of gas for the car, the mortgage was continuously late and then BANKRUPTCY. I had to make a decision that was and still is going to have an adverse effect on my credit. Let me say right here: BUT GOD.

Lessons in the paycheck to paycheck mentality had more to do with life and not just finances, but that's another message all in itself! Making decisions based on bad decisions changes your thought patterns, especially if you are not totally rooted in the LORD. I was totally distraught and there I sat building wealth, still at the J O B, but no longer living PAYCHECK TO PAYCHECK. What does that mean for you?

This means, if you are an entrepreneur and also working a job, you are leaning on your bi-weekly paycheck to get you through. This is a crutch and what I call bondage to the system. You have to work your business as if you don't have a job. Your paycheck hasn't even been established yet, because you haven't created a system for making money IN YOUR BUSINESS.

The first step to this is creating a financial worksheet; this worksheet will have every service and/or product that you have and how much of them you need to sell per week to give you the income you have on your job. You have to deduct office space rentals, inventory costs, and more to get to this understanding. Paycheck to Paycheck should no longer be an option.

www.coachdana.biz

Product/ Service	Inventory	Monthly Quota	
Publishing	Unlimited	$2,000	10 clients
Coaching	Unlimited	$2,000	5 Clients
Sell Ebooks	Unlimited	$1,000	1000 orders

Product/ Service	Inventory	Monthly Quota	
Direct Sales Company	n/a	$500	10 Clients
Direct Sales Company		$1,000	sales

www.coachdana.biz

Bankruptcy Isn't The Option

This chapter is going to be relatively short. Why? Bankruptcy is not a scriptural option for getting out of debt and becoming financially free. The word of God says we will reap what we have sown. I didn't. I wanted what was best for my household. I wanted to go with what was best and suggested by my husband. I didn't take one minute to think; I was trying to be submissive and be the WIFE. Let me tell you, if your husband is not following the Lord that doesn't mean you follow the devil. Being a loving wife to the man that doesn't know the LORD doesn't mean let him lead you down a path of self destruction, and the same for husband with your wives. We as saints cannot suggest what is wrong and get the RIGHT results.

I was so lost and didn't even try to pray. I was not even trying to stop and do what was spiritually right. I should have suffered, I should have given up on what I wanted at that time, which was nothing and I should have just paid the people that needed to be paid instead of filing for bankruptcy. Because, even after filing, I had to suffer the consequences of what I had done TWICE NOW, and play catch up. How am I an expert at helping you, when just a few short years ago, I couldn't help myself? I know now my mistakes and how it affected my house and now my mind, BUT NOT my future.

Even though I made a mistake in filing, God has place some things in my path to put me back on track. I have to tell you that really, you can't use the world's way out as your way out of your victimology in your finances, you have to reach out to the Lord and LISTEN TO HIM; believe and receive that you can have B.A.D. Money.

Note: Wives, your husband is the head of the house; he must be honored and respected, but if what he wants to do goes against the word of God, lovingly you must say its wrong.

Wives, don't you suggest anything that goes against the word of the Lord either.

www.coachdana.biz

God wants you to have wealth.

I guess you have been waiting on the lessons and the scriptures? I want to interject here that you need to study to show yourself approved. If you walk with your Bible, either in your car or on your cell phone, you have it at your finger tips to pick up and study. Now, with that housekeeping out of the way, I will share with you the word of God that says HE WANTS TO BLESS YOU.

Why am I sharing this with you? Because there are some people out there that are teaching that humble means broke, or saved, sanctified and filled with the Holy Ghost means living at or below the poverty level (anything more than that they think leaders are stealing from the church), and this is not so.

Deuteronomy 8:18
New King James Version (NKJV)
18 "And you shall remember the Lord your God, for it is He who gives you power to get wealth, that He may establish His covenant which He swore to your fathers, as it is this day.

3 John 1:2
New King James Version (NKJV)
2 Beloved, I pray that you may prosper in all things and be in health, just as your soul prospers.

There are many scriptures on prosperity and abundance, but you have to understand that you can't have any of that unless you are living wholeheartedly for God; you have to be a true servant sold out for Jesus. You can't be B.A.D (Blessed, Anointed and Destined) by serving the devil, even in finances.

The Bible does state that gifts come without repentance, but you have to use them for God's glory in order to get HIS BLESSINGS. The verse in 3 John 1 tells us this in very few words; …just as your soul prospers means you are creating a relationship with the Father that will manifest in your daily life and show others who God is in and with you.

Isaiah 45:2-3
New King James Version (NKJV)
2 'I will go before you and make the crooked places straight;
I will break in pieces the gates of bronze And cut the bars of iron.
3 I will give you the treasures of darkness And hidden riches of secret places, That you may know that I, the Lord, Who call you by your name, Am the God of Israel.

God wants to see you blessed and not cursed. I encourage you to read Deuteronomy Chapter 28; the entire chapter will give you an understanding of the blessings if you obey His word and do what He says and also gives you understand of the curses.

The lesson to be learned here is that God wants you to prosper even while a servant (pastor, apostle, bishop, evangelist, and missionary) in ministry. Just don't let money rule your life or it becomes your god.

1 Timothy 6:10
New King James Version (NKJV)
10 For the love of money is a root of all kinds of evil, for which some have strayed from the faith in their greediness, and pierced themselves through with many sorrows.

This is not the place to go wild like some of the prosperity pastors might in their sermons. This is the place to actually tell you the truth about the money you have and what you can do with it.

1. Tithe; AS GOD LEADS YOU TO TITHE. This means you have tithe where you are being prayed for and cared for; where the fruit is ripe and ready and is shared freely. People say tithe in your church home, when actually God said tithe, so DO IT!
2. Be a servant of the Lord. This means you must be willing to let your mess be a message for others. This book is prime example of that; I messed up my money and I'm helping you how not to do that.
3. Invest in ways that may not seem the norm.
4. Study scripture on wealth and money and truly get an understanding of what part you play; what part your heart plays

in it as well. Your soul must already be in place for you to even fathom what God wants to do in and through you.

From Victim to Victor: You're B.A.D

We are now at the point of the book where you must understand that you will either soar like an eagle or fall flat.

You have to get so on top of your money that you smother it to death and sweat all over it. I truly mean that when you count your pennies you are counting ever last cent! Right down to the very last decimal point.

It's scary to try to have money when all the bills have to be paid. It's scary to look at your paycheck and realize that it's your only money until the next pay check. It's hard. Why? Because you haven't placed a demand on your money to make it give you a return.

How can you go from victim to victor without having someone garnish your check? (Now, I need you to look at this chapter in two ways: as the employee and as the entrepreneur.) As an entrepreneur, you can sell more, increase your clientele, and utilize your resources to increase your income. As an employee, you have to create a plan that helps you get close to a budget; which should allow you to save money daily and not just monthly. This is how you know you are B.A.D.(Blessed, Anointed & Destined) : you have the blessing in the gifts, the anointing to do what is necessary to get to your destiny.

The root of all evil is the LOVE OF MONEY not money itself. In previous chapters, you have seen how money should serve you, not you become a slave to it. So know this, being a victor takes planning and giving up of self.

Take the time to save a $1 a day. Why? One dollar leads to more dollars, and more dollars leads to increase in your own savings, which in turn makes you the victor, not the victim. Here are a few rules of thumb from the lay person's perspective:

- ❖ KEEP CASH ON HAND NO MATTER WHAT
- ❖ TAKE INVENTORY OF WHAT YOU HAVE AND WHAT YOU NEED

- ❖ NEVER TRUST EVERYONE HIGHER THAN YOU (banks, finance advisors, etc)

- ❖ ALWAYS OVER ESTIMATE YOUR END FINANCIAL RESULT

- ❖ TRUST THE BIBLE AT ALL TIMES

You're B.A.D.

About the author

Well there isn't much I can say about myself except I'm a servant. Yes, I'm speaking in first person, which is odd in this part of the book, but the truth is, I'm here to serve from a lay person's perspective (I said that in the book, too). I'm not a financial advisor, I don't have a degree in accounting, and I'm not a banker; I invest my time in learning from the mistakes I've made and share my results with people like you. Why? Because, for the cost of this book,

www.coachdana.biz

I've made you a victor over you money, and pushed you pass bankruptcy. So, there you have it. This author is not part of the norm and never will be. Are you ready? Well, you must be, you've finished this book, the last in the series! God bless!

YOU ARE NO LONGER A VICTIM, TO ANYTHING!

www.coachdana.biz

www.ingramcontent.com/pod-product-compliance
Lightning Source LLC
Chambersburg PA
CBHW071803040426
42446CB00012B/2686